W9-AJK-894

Table of Contents

Fundamental Phonics Basics **CD-3726** Printed in the United States of America ISBN 0-88724-444-0

About the book...

This book is just one in our Best Value™ series of reproducible, skill oriented activity books. Each book is developmentally appropriate and contains over 100 pages packed with educationally sound classroom-tested activities. Each book also contains free skill cards and resource pages filled with extended activity ideas.

The activities in this book have been developed to help students master the basic skills necessary to succeed in reading. The activities have been sequenced to help insure successful completion of the assigned tasks, thus building positive self-esteem as well as the self-confidence students need to meet academic and social challenges.

The activities may be used by themselves, as supplemental activities, or as enrichment material for the reading program.

Developed by teachers and tested by students, we never lost sight of the fact that if students don't stay motivated and involved, they will never truly grasp the skills being taught on a cognitive level.

About the authors...

Patricia Pedigo has many years of teaching experience in urban, rural, public, and private settings. She has taught at all elementary and middle school grade levels, and as a reading specialist. Patricia has created many of the materials that she uses in her classroom, using a blend of content area topics with language development methods. She holds an M.Ed. in Reading Education and is nearing completion of her doctoral studies.

Dr. Roger DeSanti has been an educator since the mid 1970's. His teaching experiences have spanned a wide range of grade and ability levels from deaf nursery school through university graduate school. As a professor, he has authored numerous articles, books, achievement tests, and instructional materials.

Senior Editors: Patricia Pedigo and Roger De Santi
Production Director: Homer Desrochers
Production: Roselyn Desrochers and Debra Ollier

Ready-To-Use Ideas and Activities

The activities in this book will help children master the basic skills necessary to become competent learners. Remember, as you read through the activities listed below and as you go through this book, that all children learn at their own rate. Although repetition is important, it is critical that we never lose sight of the fact that it is equally important to build children's self-esteem and self-confidence if we want them to become successful learners.

Flashcard ideas
The back of this book has removable flash cards that will be great for basic skill and enrichment activities. Pull the flash cards out and cut them apart (if you have access to a paper cutter, use that). Following are several ideas for use of the flashcards.

★ Help the student to learn to read the flash cards by flashing a few words at a time. Give the student ten seconds to say the word. Allow him/her to "keep" the recognized words. As the child becomes more proficient with recognition, shorten the time limit.

★ Have the students find flashcard words that follow a rule relating to the phonics concept being taught. For example, if you are discussing "short e" words, have the student find all the "short e" words in the pack of flashcards.

★ Have the student classify the flashcards according to their beginning sounds.

★ Have the student classify the flashcards according to their ending sounds.

★ Have the student classify the flashcards according to their vowel sounds (a, e, i, o, or u).

★ As the child becomes familiar with the various vowel sounds, have him/her sort the pack of cards into like sounds (i.e. long a, short e, long i, etc.)

★ Sort the flashcards into groups or categories that the children select. They may begin with very general categories (animals, people, things we do, nouns, things that are alive, etc.). As the children become more proficient, guide them toward more specific categories that require higher thinking skills (i.e. things people use, things that cannot move, tools, words that describe, etc.)

Ready-To-Use Ideas and Activities

★ Give the child a small group of cards with a common form (i.e. long a words). Allow the child to "keep" the cards for two or three days. He/she may practice reading the cards during spare time. Quiz the child on the cards at the end of the specified time limit.

★ Divide the cards into small groups and have children alphabetize them.

★ As the child grows proficient at word recognition, have them alphabetize the entire pack of flashcards.

★ Have students locate flash card words in books, magazines, and/or newspapers.

★ Have students draw pictures to illustrate the flash cards.

★ Students can copy the flashcard words into a journal of "Words I Know" as they demonstrate recognition mastery.

★ Use the flash cards to show similarities in sounds. (For example: "oa" and "o consonant silent e" can make the same sound).

★ Divide the flash cards into groups of vowel-consonant patterns (I.E. CVCV, CVVC, CCVC, etc.).

★ Students may make a book of any skill being discussed. They can illustrate the book with pictures from magazines or newspapers. For example, a book of "Short O Words" may include pictures of a mop, top, sock, box, clock, etc.)

★ As the child demonstrates recognition of the words, select a related group of cards and have the child make sentences for each.

★ Have the child select two or three cards that can be related in some way (i.e. bed, big, and sleep). The child should write a sentence using the words in context. (i.e. I sleep in a big bed).

★ Select a group of five to ten words. Have the child create a paragraph or story that uses each of the words in context.

★ Have the child select words to use in a written paragraph or story.

★ Have the student illustrate the cards using pictures they find in magazines or pictures they draw themselves. Use the pictures to create rebus stories. Create separate flashcards with pictures that illustrate each of the flashcard words. Have the child match the word with the picture.

Ready-To-Use Ideas and Activities

★ Use the picture and word flashcards to play "Match-Up". Select a group of ten to fifteen flashcard words and their matching pictures. Shuffle the words and place them face down in two or three rows. Repeat with the picture cards, placing the rows near the word cards. Taking turns, each player selects one word card and one picture card. The player turns these two cards face up. If the word matches the picture, the player may keep the cards and take another turn. If the cards do not match, the player returns them to the face down position and the next player takes a turn. Play continues until all the matches have been claimed. The player with the most matches is the winner.

★ Play several variations on the "Match-Up" game described above:
1) Sort the flashcards into groups of long and short vowels. Shuffle all the cards and lay them in rows face down on the table. Matches are any two long vowel or any two short vowel words.
2) Matches must be like vowels (i.e. two "long a" words, two "short o" words, etc.)
3) Match the cards according to same initial or final consonant sounds.

★ Use the picture and word flashcards to play "Go Fish". Shuffle the deck and deal six cards to each player. Place the remainder of the deck face down in the middle of the table. The first player (A) asks another player (B) for any words that begin with a consonant sound (i.e. the letter "d"). If player B has such a card it must be surrendered to player A. If a match is made, player A continues. If no match is made, player A must draw a card from the table. If the match is made from the table, player A takes another turn. If no match is made, the next player takes a turn. The first player to match all the cards in his/her hand wins.

★ Play variations on the "Go Fish" game described above:
1) Play for matches of final consonant sounds.
2) Match the cards according to like vowel sounds (a, e, i, o, or u).
3) Match the cards according to specific vowels (i.e. short "a", long "u", etc.)

★ Have the students find pictures of items they like in a magazine or catalogue. Cut out the pictures and paste them on a poster board. Identify the vowel sound(s) in the name of each picture. Variations: Select a theme such as toys or favorite foods. Have the students draw or find pictures that illustrate their choices. Identify the correct vowel sound(s) heard in each word.

★ Choose three to five flashcards as "Words for the Day" or "Words for the Week". Use any of the activities to reinforce those words.

Name_____

Write each word three times.

bat _____

cat _____

fat _____

mat _____

can _____

fan _____

man _____

pan _____

Name _____

Cut out the pictures. Paste them next to the correct words.

can   cat

bat   man

pan   mat

fan   hat

Name _____

Unscramble the words and write them on the lines.

t m a	a h t
_____	_____
a n m	p n a
_____	_____
n f a	a c t
_____	_____
t a b	n a c
_____	_____

Circle the words that are not used above.

fat	ban	rat	can	man
fan	mat	cat	bat	van
hat	sat	pan	tan	ran

Name _____

Write each word three times.

bag _____

rag _____

tag _____

wag _____

ball _____

fall _____

tall _____

wall _____

Name _____

Cut out the pictures. Paste them next to the correct words.

fall   tag

bag   tall

wall   wag

ball   rag

Name _____

Unscramble the words and write them on the lines.

t g a	a l l t
b l a l	g a w
a b g	l l f a
w l a l	r g a

Circle the words that are not used above.

call	ball	rag	mall	wall
bag	small	wag	tall	tag
sag	fall	sag	hall	hag

Name _____

Write each word three times.

hen _____

men _____

pen _____

ten _____

jet _____

net _____

pet _____

wet _____

CD-3726

Name _____

Cut out the pictures. Paste them next to the correct words.

pet   men

ten   jet

wet   hen

pen   net

Name _____

Unscramble the words and write them on the lines.

t j e	p n e
t e p	e n t
n m e	e w t
n e h	n t e

Circle the words that are not used above.

jet	den	Ben	wet	men
ten	pen	net	then	pet
set	met	bet	hen	get

Name _____

Write each word three times.

bed _____

fed _____

Ted _____

sled _____

bell _____

fell _____

well _____

yell _____

Name _____

Cut out the pictures. Paste them next to the correct words.

sled

well

bell

fed

bed

yell

fell

Ted

Name _____

Unscramble the words and write them on the lines.

e s l d	e l y l
l f e l	b d e
d e r	b l e l
l l w e	e d f

Circle the words that are not used above.

Ted	red	led	well	bed
sled	bell	sell	fell	cell
tell	fed	Ned	wed	yell

CD-3726

_____

Name _____

Write each word three times.

→ fin _____

pin _____

tin _____

win _____

big _____

dig _____

pig _____

wig _____

Name _____

Cut out the pictures. Paste them next to the correct words.

dig   pin

tin   pig

big   win

fin   wig

Name _____

Unscramble the words and write them on the lines.

g i p	i n f
n w i	b g i
g w i	n i p
i n t	d g i

Circle the words that are not used above.

fig	big	grin	tin	rig
win	pin	twin	dig	zig
spin	wig	pig	twig	fin

 CD-3726

Name _____

Write each word three times.

hip

_____
- -
_____

lip

_____
- -
_____

rip

_____
- -
_____

zip

_____
- -
_____

bill

_____
- -
_____

fill

_____
- -
_____

hill

_____
- -
_____

pill

_____
- -
_____

Name _____

Cut out the pictures. Paste them next to the correct words.

lip   fill

hill   hip

rip   bill

pill   zip

Name _____

Unscramble the words and write them on the lines.

l i b l	p i r
p h i	i l l f
l h i l	i p l
p z i	p l l i

Circle the words that are not used above.

pill	zip	hip	dill	hill
will	tip	mill	bill	dip
nip	fill	rip	gill	lip

18   CD-3726

Name _____

Write each word three times.

cot _____

dot _____

hot _____

pot _____

hop _____

mop _____

pop _____

top _____

Name _____

Cut out the pictures. Paste them next to the correct words.

hot   hop

mop   dot

cot   top

pop   pot

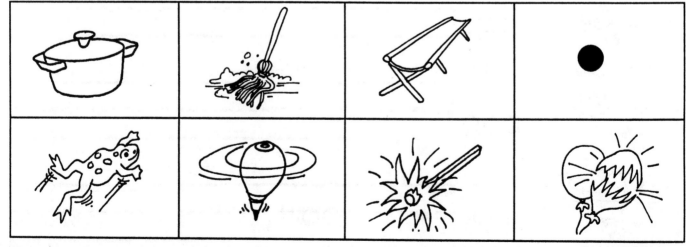

20

Name _____

Unscramble the words and write them on the lines.

p t o	o p p
t h o	t o d
p h o	t c o
o p t	o m p

Circle the words that are not used above.

pop	cot	got	hop	jot
bop	mop	cop	dot	lot
pot	hot	top	not	stop

Name _____

Write each word three times.

dog

hog

jog

log

Bob

cob

rob

sob

Name _____

Cut out the pictures. Paste them next to the correct words.

cob   hog

log   rob

Bob   jog

dog   sob

Name _____

Unscramble the words and write them on the lines.

o r b	g j o
o g h	b B o
b o s	b o c
o g l	g d o

Circle the words that are not used above.

dog	mob	rob	fog	gob
bog	clog	hog	cob	job
sob	log	slob	Bob	jog

Name _____

Write each word three times.

cub _____

rub _____

sub _____

tub _____

bug _____

jug _____

rug _____

tug _____

 CD-3726

Name _____

Cut out the pictures. Paste them next to the correct words.

bug   tub

sub   jug

rug   rub

cub   tug

Name _____

Unscramble the words and write them on the lines.

u g r	b u r
g b u	b t u
b u s	u g j
t g u	u c b

Circle the words that are not used above.

nub	bug	rub	dug	pub
cub	hug	jug	hub	sub
tug	tub	lug	rug	mug

Name _____

Write each word three times.

gum _____

drum _____

mum _____

plum _____

bump _____

hump _____

jump _____

pump _____

Name _____

Cut out the pictures. Paste them next to the correct words.

jump

drum

gum

bump

hump

plum

mum

pump

Name _____

Unscramble the words and write them on the lines.

m l u p	p u p m
_____	_____
m u j p	m u g
_____	_____
u m d r	p m b u
_____	_____
m m u	m u h p
_____	_____

Circle the words that are not used above.

plum	drum	dump	jump	bum
bump	chum	lump	gum	sum
stump	hump	mum	hum	pump

CD-3726

Name _____

Write each word three times.

face _____

lace _____

race _____

space _____

bake _____

cake _____

lake _____

rake _____

CD-3726

Name _____

Cut out the pictures. Match them to the words and paste.

space   rake

cake   lace

race   bake

lake   face

Name _____

Unscramble the words and write them on the lines.

c e a k	a c e f
k l a e	c e a r
c a l e	a k e r
k e a b	s c a e p

Circle the words that were not used above.

face	bake	pace	fake	race
place	rake	make	ace	lake
space	sake	lace	cake	take

Name _____

Write each word three times.

gate _____

mate _____

plate _____

skate _____

mail _____

nail _____

pail _____

sail _____

CD-3726

Name _____

Cut out the pictures. Match them to the words and paste.

pail

mate

skate

mail

nail

plate

gate

sail

Name _____

Unscramble the words and write them on the lines.

t e m a	a n i l
a p l i	l a s i
t l a p e	t a g e
m a l i	k a s t e

Circle the words that were not used above.

skate	mail	date	fate	late
hate	sail	gate	bail	fail
plate	hail	mate	nail	pail

Name _____

Write each word three times.

beam _____

dream _____

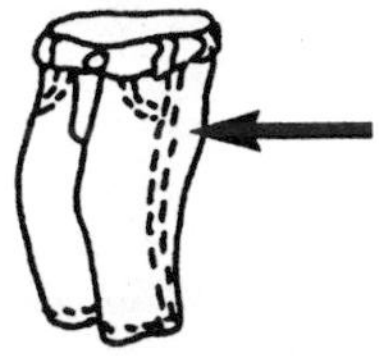

seam _____

team _____

fear _____

hear _____

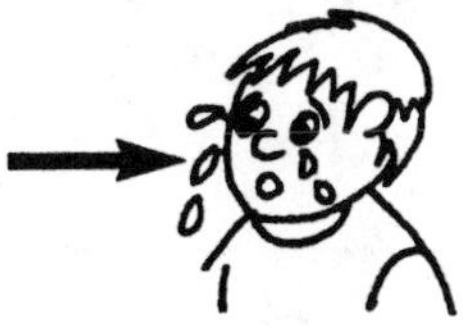

tear _____

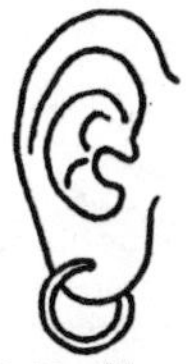

ear _____

CD-3726

Name _____

Cut out the pictures. Match them to the words and paste.

seam   hear

ear   team

dream   fear

tear   beam

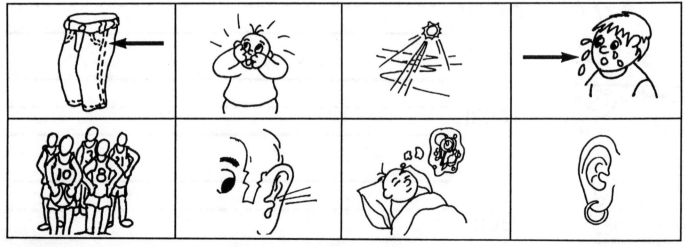

Name _____

Unscramble the words and write them on the lines.

r e t a	a e s m
r e a f	m e a r d
y r e a	a h e r
t a e m	m a e b

Circle the words that were not used above.

fear	cream	seam	gear	near
dear	beam	steam	year	ear
dream	hear	tear	clear	team

Name _____

Write each word three times.

reed _____

seed _____

speed _____

weed _____

deep _____

jeep _____

sheep _____

sleep _____

Name _____

Cut out the pictures. Match them to the words and paste.

seed   jeep

sheep   speed

weed   deep

sleep   reed

Name _____

Unscramble the words and write them on the lines.

e e h s p	e e s d
e p d e	d e r e
s e p e d	w e d e
l e p e s	p e j e

Circle the words that were not used above.

weed	deed	deep	keep	seed
feed	speed	peep	need	seep
heed	sheep	reed	sleep	jeep

Skill: long i words -ice -ine

Name ____________________

Write each word three times.

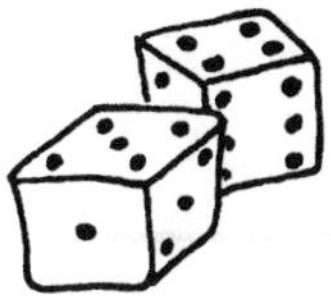

dice

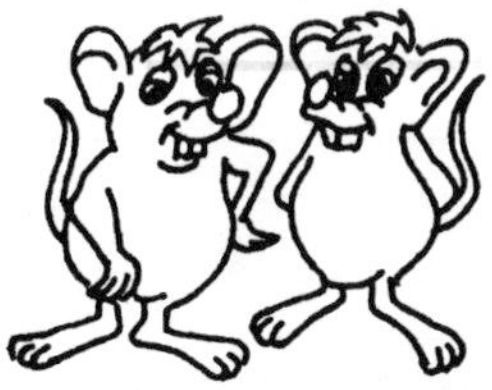

mice

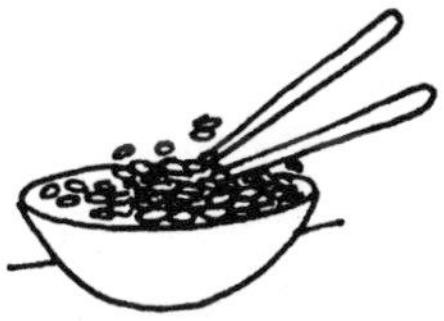

rice

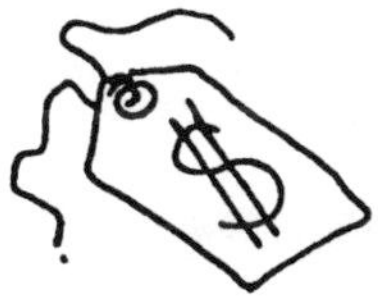

price

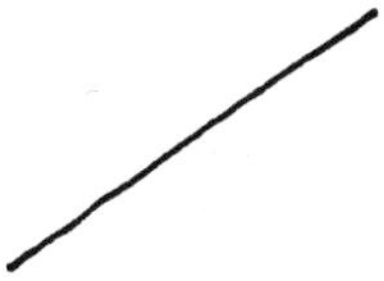

line

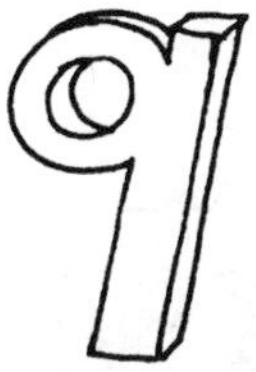

nine

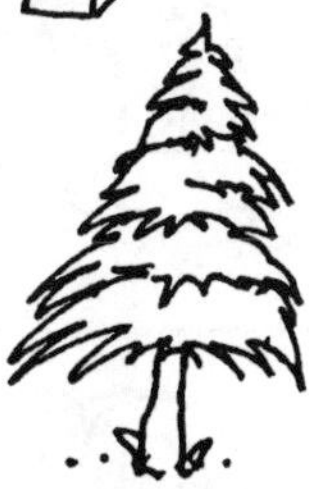

pine

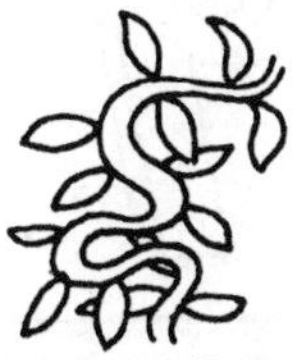

vine

Name_____

Cut out the pictures. Match them to the words and paste.

line   rice

dice   pine

nine   price

mice   vine

Name _____

Unscramble the words and write them on the lines.

n e v i	c r i e
d e i c	i n n e
n i p e	p i e r c
i c e m	n i l e

Circle the words that were not used above.

pine	fine	dice	nice	mine
ice	line	slice	wine	vine
price	dine	nine	mice	rice

Name _____

Write each word three times.

dive _____

drive _____

five _____

hive _____

hide _____

ride _____

slide _____

tide _____

   CD-3726

Name _____

Cut out the pictures. Match them to the words and paste.

tide   hive

drive   hide

ride   five

dive   slide

Name _____

Unscramble the words and write them on the lines.

d i l s e	v i f e
e d i w	d i r e
e v i h	v i r e d
d i e h	e i v d

Circle the words that were not used above.

wide	hive	live	pride	alive
side	five	slide	tide	dive
drive	ride	bride	hide	chive

Name _____

Write each word three times.

boat _____

coat _____

goat _____

moat _____

cold _____

fold _____

gold _____

hold _____

49

CD-3726

Name _____

Cut out the pictures. Match them to the words and paste.

gold   goat

boat   fold

hold   moat

coat   cold

Name _____

Unscramble the words and write them on the lines.

t o c a	d o l f
a t o b	o a t m
o l d h	l o c d
t o a g	d o l g

Circle the words that were not used above.

float	gold	oat	moat	cold
boat	told	coat	hold	bold
mold	fold	goat	sold	old

Name _____

Write each word three times.

bone _____

cone _____

phone _____

stone _____

core _____

tore _____

shore _____

store _____

Name _____

Cut out the pictures. Match them to the words and paste.

tore   phone

bone   store

core   stone

cone   shore

Name _____

Unscramble the words and write them on the lines.

n o p h e	r o c e
o n c e	t r o e
s o h e r	o n s e t
o r t e s	n e o b

Circle the words that were not used above.

bone	more	pore	lore	stone
core	cone	shore	lone	tone
phone	tore	sore	store	bore

Name _____

Write each word three times.

cube _____

flute _____

fruit _____

fuel _____

huge _____

mule _____

music _____

ruler _____

Name _____

Cut out the pictures. Match them to the words and paste.

fuel

flute

music

ruler

mule

cube

huge

fruit

Name _____

Unscramble the words and write them on the lines.

u h g e	l u e m
_____ - - - - - - _____	_____ - - - - - - _____
t i u f r	t u c e
_____ - - - - - - _____	_____ - - - - - - _____
b c e u	s c u i m
_____ - - - - - - _____	_____ - - - - - - _____
l e f u	l e r u r
_____ - - - - - - _____	_____ - - - - - - _____

Circle the words that were not used above.

fuel	cube	use	fruit	rule
fume	music	fuse	ruler	mule
future	cute	huge	fume	plume

Name _____

Write each word three times.

blue _____

cute _____

glue _____

prune _____

suit _____

super _____

tube _____

tune _____

Name _____

Cut out the pictures. Match them to the words and paste.

tune   glue

super   prune

blue   tube

cute   suit

Name _____

Unscramble the words and write them on the lines.

t n u e	u l g e
p r u s e	n u p r e
e u b l	u i t s
b u t e	t u f l e

Circle the words that were not used above.

flute	tuna	ruin	glue	prune
dune	rude	tune	duty	future
suit	tube	blue	human	super

Name _____

Write the missing vowel for each picture.

b __ t	h __ n	f __ n
c __ t	c __ b	c __ n
j __ t	b __ g	h __ p
b __ g	b __ g	b __ d

61   CD-3726

Name _____

Write the missing vowel for each picture.

h __ p	d __ g	g __ m
b __ ll	b __ ll	h __ t
t __ n	b __ mp	c __ t
m __ n	p __ n	d __ t

Name _____

Write the missing vowel for each picture.

r __ b   f __ n   n __ t

d __ g   m __ p   j __ g

r __ g   f __ d   l __ p

h __ g   d r __ m   f __ ll

Name _____

Write the missing vowel for each picture.

f __ ll	f __ ll	c __ b
h __ m p	f __ t	p __ n
t __ n	h __ t	s __ b
m __ n	p __ t	p __ g

64 CD-3726

Name _____

Write the missing vowel for each picture.

p __ p   r __ g   t __ g

r __ d   r __ p   j __ g

m __ m   t __ ll   w __ ll

h __ ll   r __ b   j __ m p

Name _____

Write the missing vowel for each picture.

f __ ce	b __ am	d __ ce
b __ at	c __ be	b __ ke
f __ ar	l __ ne	c __ ld
h __ ge	g __ te	r __ ed

66

Name _____

Write the missing vowel for each picture.

d __ ve	b __ ne	bl __ e
m __ il	d __ ep	h __ de
c __ re	s __ it	l __ ce
dr __ am	m __ ce	c __ at

67 CD-3726

Name _____

Write the missing vowel for each picture.

c __ te	c __ __ ke	h __ __ ar
n __ __ ne	f __ __ ld	m __ __ le
m __ __ te	s __ __ ed	dr __ __ ve
c __ __ ne	fl __ __ te	n __ __ il

Name _____

Write the missing vowel for each picture.

j__ep	r__de	t__re
s__per	r__ce	s__am
r__ce	g__at	fr__it
l__ke	t__ar	p__ne

Name _____

Write the missing vowel for each picture.

g __ ld

m __ sic

sp __ ed

f __ ve

ph __ ne

gl __ e

p __ il

sh __ ep

sl __ de

c __ re

t __ be

pl __ te

Name _____

Write the missing vowel for each picture.

w __ n	sp ___ c e	p __ t
t ___ a m	t __ b	p r ___ c e
p __ n	m ___ a t	w __ t
f ___ e l	w ___ g	r ___ k e

Name _____

Write the missing vowel for each picture.

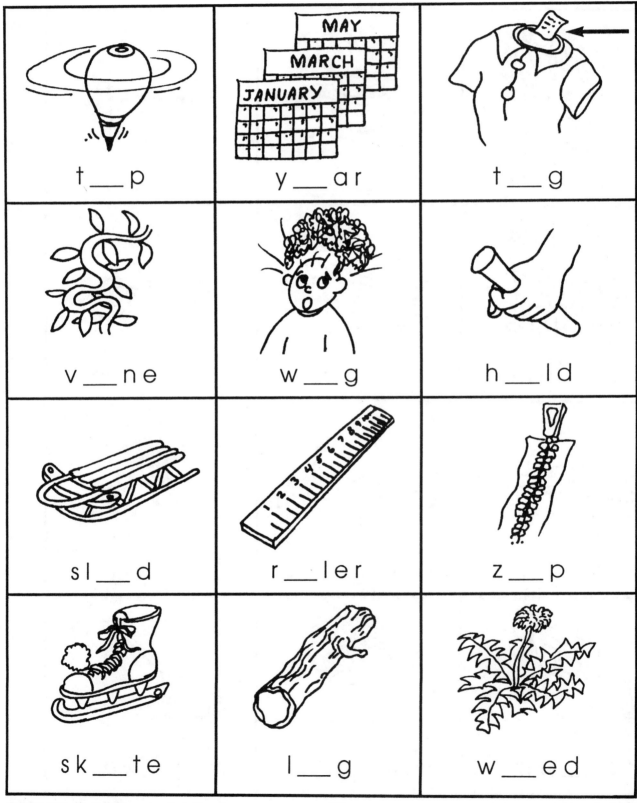

t __ p

y __ a r

t __ g

v __ n e

w __ g

h __ l d

s l __ d

r __ l e r

z __ p

s k __ t e

l __ g

w __ e d

Name _____

Write the missing vowel for each picture.

pl __ m	h __ ve	w __ ll
st __ ne	y __ ll	pr __ ne
p __ ll	s __ il	s __ b
sl __ ep	p __ mp	st __ re

Name _____

Choose the answer that makes sense then write it on the line.

1. A _____ can fly.   **bat**   **cat**

2. Please _____ my back.   **rib**   **rub**

3. That _____ is my father.   **men**   **man**

4. It is _____ today.   **hot**   **hat**

5. Put the lunch in a _____ .   **big**   **bag**

6. I will _____ to school.   **jog**   **jug**

7. Some apples are _____ .   **red**   **rod**

8. Play _____ with me.   **ball**   **bell**

9. My _____ is a dog.   **pat**   **pet**

10. The puppy will _____ his tail.   **wig**   **wag**

Write the answers that have a short a sound here.

Name _____

Choose the answer that makes sense then write it on the line.

1. Do not _____ down!   **fall**   **fell**

2. A fish has a _____ .   **fun**   **fin**

3. A _____ ate the cheese.   **sat**   **rat**

4. Do not _____ my paper.   **rip**   **lip**

5. A _____ makes wind.   **fin**   **fan**

6. A camel has one _____ .   **hump**   **jump**

7. A rabbit can _____ .   **hop**   **hip**

8. I can _____ a big hole.   **dig**   **dug**

9. I play a _____ in the band.   **gum**   **drum**

10. I will _____ the race.   **won**   **win**

Write the answers that have a short a sound here.

Name _____

Choose the answer that makes sense then write it on the line.

1. The _____ is on the floor.   **rug**   **rag**

2. Are you feeling _____ ?   **well**   **will**

3. That is a _____ tree.   **tell**   **tall**

4. A _____ flys over clouds.   **jot**   **jet**

5. The _____ has two chicks.   **hen**   **men**

6. Spot is the name of my _____.   **dig**   **dog**

7. I got _____ in the rain.   **wet**   **met**

8. _____ my cup to the top.   **Fill**   **Fall**

9. I will go to _____ now.   **bed**   **bad**

10. Fry the eggs in that _____ .   **pin**   **pan**

Write the answers that have a short e sound here.

Name _____

Choose the answer that makes sense then write it on the line.

1. We _____ the horse oats.   **fed**   **bed**

2. Ring the _____ .   **ball**   **bell**

3. Let's play _____ .   **bag**   **tag**

4. I like corn on the _____ .   **cob**   **mob**

5. Put a _____ on the fire.   **log**   **jog**

6. I will eat a_____.   **mum**   **plum**

7. Can you _____very high?   **jump**   **stump**

8. That is a _____ ball!   **beg**   **big**

9. Mother will _____the floor.   **stop**   **mop**

10. My _____ is in the tent.   **cot**   **cut**

Write the answers that have a short e sound here.

Name _____

Choose the answer that makes sense then write it on the line.

1. A _____ just flew by.	**big**	**bug**
2. Let's climb that _____.	**hill**	**hall**
3. My _____ goes in the snow.	**slid**	**sled**
4. Joe just _____ down.	**fell**	**fill**
5. Do not _____ at me.	**yell**	**bell**
6. We wash in the _____.	**tab**	**tub**
7. I _____ my head.	**bumped**	**jumped**
8. Put it on _____ of this.	**tap**	**top**
9. I have a _____ cat.	**pit**	**pet**
10. I _____ when I get hurt.	**mob**	**sob**

Write the answers that have a short i sound here.

Name _____

Choose the answer that makes sense then write it on the line.

1. A _____ can make you well.   **hill**   **pill**

2. Put a _____ over the letter i.   **pot**   **dot**

3. The dog _____ on a rope.   **bugs**   **tugs**

4. _____ the zipper.   **Zip**   **Sip**

5. A _____ is part of a leg.   **hip**   **hop**

6. This old shirt is a _____ .   **rag**   **rig**

7. I have _____ toes.   **tin**   **ten**

8. I like to drink _____ .   **pup**   **pop**

9. Cook soup in a big _____ .   **pet**   **pot**

10. That lady wears a _____ .   **wag**   **wig**

Write the answers that have a short o sound here.

Name _____

Choose the answer that makes sense then write it on the line.

1. A _____ is an animal. pig   peg

2. I bit my _____ ! lap   lip

3. A _____ is a flower mum   gum

4. A _____ is a baby bear. cub   cab

5. Boys grow up to be _____. men   hen

6. I blow bubbles with _____. gum   hum

7. I have a butterfly _____ . net   nut

8. Use a _____ , not a pencil. ten   pen

9. A _____ goes under water. sob   sub

10. _____ air into my bike tires. Pump   Lump

Write the answers that have a short u sound here.

Name _____

Choose the answer that makes sense then write it on the line.

1. _____ the wood together.   **Sail**   **Nail**

2. Leaves grow on a _____ .   **mine**   **vine**

3. _____ grow into plants.   **Needs**   **Seeds**

4. _____ the cake in the oven.   **Bake**   **Bike**

5. The ice cream is _____ .   **cold**   **fold**

6. The _____ is ringing.   **cone**   **phone**

7. I like _____ with my dinner.   **race**   **rice**

8. You did a _____ job!   **super**   **fruit**

9. Put your food on a _____ .   **gate**   **plate**

10. Let's have a _____ .   **face**   **race**

Write the answers that have a long a sound here.

Name _____

Choose the answer that makes sense then write it on the line.

1. My nose is on my _____ .   lace   face

2. I like to _____ on a sled.   slide   wide

3. Do not eat the apple _____ .   care   core

4. A_____ helps us draw a line.   ruler   super

5. Help me _____ this sheet.   cold   fold

6. We can_____ the leaves.   cake   rake

7. How_____ is the box?   side   wide

8. Let's swim in the_____ .   lake   make

9. I am _____ years old.   fine   nine

10. Put the water in a _____ .   pail   mail

Write the answers that have a long a sound here.

Name _____

Choose the answer that makes sense then write it on the line.

1. I had a _____ last night.   **dream**   **seam**

2. The _____ are in the barn.   **sheep**   **sleep**

3. That boat has a _____ .   **sail**   **tail**

4. Stars are out in _____ .   **spice**   **space**

5. A _____ is a small rock.   **bone**   **stone**

6. Roll the _____ and play.   **dice**   **slice**

7. I _____ we may be late.   **tear**   **fear**

8. I like chocolate _____ .   **cake**   **make**

9. _____ and I will find you.   **Side**   **Hide**

10. My paper _____ in half.   **tore**   **tire**

Write the answers that have a long e sound here.

Name _____

Choose the answer that makes sense then write it on the line.

1. I can _____ into the pool.   **five**   **dive**

2. Do you _____ the band?   **hear**   **tear**

3. A _____ is like a horse.   **mule**   **mile**

4. My ring is made of _____ .   **gold**   **hold**

5. I have _____ dimes.   **five**   **dive**

6. Sally is one _____ old.   **dear**   **year**

7. Can you _____ a car?   **drive**   **hive**

8. Please be on my_____ .   **steam**   **team**

9. Close the barnyard _____ .   **gate**   **mate**

10. Do you play the _____ ?   **flute**   **cute**

Write the answers that have a long i sound here.

Name _____

Choose the answer that makes sense then write it on the line.

1. The _____ is on the lake.   boat   coat

2. Wear a _____ to the party.   fruit   suit

3. Please _____ this letter.   mail   pail

4. A shell was on the _____ .   shore   share

5. Let's _____ after school.   gate   skate

6. The dog has a _____ .   lone   bone

7. Do not _____ in a car.   need   speed

8. A _____ is a kind of fruit.   prune   tune

9. Draw a _____ under this.   line   pine

10. The _____ ate my lunch!   moat   goat

Write the answers that have a long o sound here.

85   CD-3726

Name _____

Choose the answer that makes sense then write it on the line.

1. That is a tall _____ tree.   **line**   **pine**

2. The paint comes in a _____ .   **cube**   **tube**

3. Use _____ to hold that.   **glue**   **blue**

4. Wear a warm _____ today.   **coat**   **boat**

5. May I _____ your bike?   **side**   **ride**

6. I think you are _____ .   **cute**   **flute**

7. Is the water very _____ ?   **keep**   **deep**

8. Please _____ the garden.   **need**   **weed**

9. I love to eat _____ .   **fruit**   **suit**

10. Gas is a kind of _____ .   **fuel**   **mule**

Write the answers that have a long u sound here.

Name _____

Choose the answer that makes sense then write it on the line.

1. I shop in that _____. store core

2. I like to listen to _____. ruler music

3. The cat does not like _____. price mice

4. I need an ice _____. cube cute

5. The bees are in their _____. drive hive

6. _____ on to my hand. Gold Hold

7. I like the color _____. blue glue

8. That shirt is _____ on you! huge tube

9. I _____ in a bed. sheep sleep

10. Play a _____ on your horn. tune prune

Write the answers that have a long u sound here.

Name _____

Put these words into the correct group.

bag	bat	bake	cake
can	fan	face	gate
mate	nail	pan	rag
rake	space	tall	wall

Short a   Long a

_____   _____

_____   _____

_____   _____

_____   _____

_____   _____

_____   _____

Choose five words and draw a picture next to each.

Name _____

Put these words into the correct group.

beam	bed	deep	fear
fell	hen	jeep	jet
men	pet	reed	sled
sleep	team	year	yell

Short e

Long e

_____

_____

_____

_____

_____

_____

_____

_____

_____

_____

_____

_____

_____

_____

Choose five words and draw a picture next to each.

Name _____

Put these words into the correct group.

bill	dice	dig	dive
fin	five	hide	hill
line	lip	pin	price
vine	wide	wig	zip

Short i

_____

_____

_____

_____

_____

_____

Long i

_____

_____

_____

_____

_____

_____

Choose five words and draw a picture next to each.

Name _____

Put these words into the correct group.

boat	cob	cone	dot
fold	goat	hold	hop
jog	log	moat	mop
phone	pot	rob	store

Short o   Long o

_____   _____

_____   _____

_____   _____

_____   _____

_____   _____

_____   _____

Choose five words and draw a picture next to each.

Name _____

Put these words into the correct group.

blue	bug	cub	cute
drum	flute	fruit	glue
gum	hump	jug	mule
rub	ruler	tug	tune

Short u   Long u

_____   _____

_____   _____

_____   _____

_____   _____

_____   _____

_____   _____

Choose five words and draw a picture next to each.

Name _____

Put these words into the correct group.

ball	bell	cat	dream
fed	hear	lake	man
net	pail	race	sheep
skate	ten	wag	weed

Short a	Short e
_____	_____
_____	_____
_____	_____

Long a	Long e
_____	_____
_____	_____
_____	_____

Name _____

Put these words into the correct group.

bone	bump	coat	core
cot	cube	dog	huge
mule	plum	rug	sob
stone	suit	top	tub

Short o	Short u
_____	_____
_____	_____
_____	_____

Long o	Long u
_____	_____
_____	_____
_____	_____

Name _____

Fill in the blanks with the short a words in the box.

Sally's Walk

Sally went for a walk down her street. She stopped in front of the house next to hers. A _____ was in the yard. He was feeding his _____. The man went into his house. The cat jumped to the top of a brick _____ that went around the yard. Sally walked on to the next yard. A dog was barking at the cat. He began to _____ his tail when he saw Sally. He got his _____ and tossed it in the air. The dog put the ball at Sally's feet and _____ down. She threw the ball and the dog went after it. He came back with a paper _____ in his mouth. A _____ on the bag said "Open Me". He gave the bag to _____ and she opened it. _____ you guess what was inside?

bag	ball	Can	cat	man
Sally	sat	tag	wag	wall

Name _____

Fill in the blanks with the short e words at the bottom of the page.

Ned

One summer day Ned went to his uncle's farm. He went

to the barnyard to look around. Ned saw a fat _____ and

her five babies. He _____ corn to the hen. There

were some sheep in a _____ near the barn. A horse and

her colt were in the barn. Ned stopped to _____ the

soft nose of the colt. Ned walked out of the barn and saw a

round stone wall. He looked over the wall and saw that it was

a wishing _____ . Ned bent over to see further into the

well and _____ in! The water was not very deep, but

Ned was all _____ . He began to _____ for help.

Two _____ came running. They used a big _____ to

pull him out. Ned laughed and said "I am all right now"!

fed	fell	hen	men	net
pen	pet	well	wet	yell

96

Name _____

Fill in the blanks with the short i words **at** the bottom of the page.

Bill's Pond

Bill was playing in his back yard. He saw a _____

pile of dirt under a bush. It was an ant _____. He had

an idea. He would make a pond for the ants to _____

in. The ants could race and see who would _____ . Bill

began to _____ a small hole next to the ant hill. He

worked on that hole for a long time.   When it was ready he

_____the hole with water. The ants came to the

pond but they did not go _____ .   Bill laughed at his

_____ idea. Ants cannot swim. They do not have

_____ like fish, but now they_____ have

a nice pond to

look at!

big	dig	filled	fins	hill
in	silly	swim	will	win

Name _____

Fill in the blanks with the short o words at the bottom of the page.

Friends

Bob and Rob are friends. They are alike in many ways.

Both boys like to climb to the _____ of the fence. Then

they _____ down. They both have a _____

for a pet. They even like the same foods. Their favorite food

is corn on the _____ . Bob and Rob like to drink

_____ chocolate in the winter and cold _____

in the summer. Both boys like to make things. Once they

made a big _____ out of clay. Another time they

made a _____ cabin out of sticks. Bob and

_____ have known each other since they were

two years old. They have been friends for a _____

time!

cob	dog	hop	hot	log
long	pop	pot	Rob	top

Name _____

Fill in the blanks with the short u words **at** the bottom of the page.

My Toy Box

I have a big box to keep my toys in.   It is painted yellow and green. My box is _____ of toys. At the bottom I keep an old red _____ for banging. Next I have three boats and one _____ to play with in the _____. On top of them I keep two stuffed animals.   One is a camel with a big _____ .   The other is a small bear _____ . On the top I keep a real animal!   It is a _____ with wings and six legs.   My toy box is so full I have to _____ on the top to open it. Sometimes I pull the top so hard it flies open and _____ my head. Then I have to _____ my head to make it feel better.

bug	bumps	cub	drum	full
hump	rub	sub	tub	tug

Name _____

Fill in the blanks with the long a words at the bottom of the page.

Amy's Party

Amy is having a party today. She _____ letters

to all her friends last week to tell them about it.   Amy has put

on her best dress. It has _____ all over it.   Her

mother has _____ a _____ for the

children to eat. They will put the cake on party _____ .

Amy has _____ many plans for her party. The

children will play _____ . They will have a running

_____ . They may even _____ boats on

the nearby pond! The doorbell rings.   It is the first guest.

Amy has a big smile on her _____ .

baked	cake	face	games	lace
made	mailed	plates	race	sail

Name _____

Fill in the blanks with the long e words **at** the bottom of the page.

A Dream by the Sea

Last week Lee went camping with her family. They went

to a camp by the sea. They knew it was a nice place

because they went there last _____. The camp has

a nice beach for swimming. _____ likes to swim in

water that is not too _____. She is not a good

swimmer. The family likes to camp by the _____.

They have a _____ to drive over the sand dunes.

They _____ in a tent. Lee likes to _____

the waves at night. One night she had a _____.

She found a large _____ and planted it. A

giant _____ grew from the seed. It became a sea

weed. What a strange dream!

dream	deep	hear	jeep	Lee
sea	seed	sleep	weed	year

Name _____

Fill in the blanks with the long i words at the bottom of the page.

The Woods

Mike and Ivan like to picnic in the woods. It takes them

only _____ minutes to get there. They like to

_____ their _____ down the trails. There

are many _____ trees in the woods. Some of them

are covered with _____ that are just right for swinging

from. One tree is so _____ the boys cannot put

their arms around it! Mike and Ivan like to _____ in

the bushes and watch for animals. They often see little

_____ gathering seeds. Once they saw some bees

going into a large _____ . The woods are

_____ with small animals that are fun to watch.

alive	bikes	five	hide	hive
pine	mice	ride	vines	wide

Name _____

Fill in the blanks with the long o words at the bottom of the page.

Gold Fish

Once a boy named Joe lived near a castle. There was a

_____ around the castle and Joe liked to fish there.

He had a small _____ to fish from. The boat

_____ on the water as Joe fished. _____

caught one fish each day for his dinner. One winter morning

it was very _____ out. Joe put on his _____

and went to the moat. His fingers were so cold he could

barely _____ the oars. He pushed away from

the _____ and began to fish. He looked down

and saw a shiny _____ in the water. Joe picked it

up and saw that it was a big piece of _____ .

He had found gold instead of a fish. What a lucky day!

boat	**coat**	**cold**	**floated**	**gold**
hold	**Joe**	**moat**	**shore**	**stone**

Name _____

Fill in the blanks with the long u words **at** the bottom of the page.

Ruth's Flute

Ruth likes school. She loves _____ class better

than anything. She plays a _____ in the band. Her

teacher says she is a _____ student. She can

play a _____ without looking at the music!

_____ is learning to write her own songs. She uses a

_____ to make the lines then draws in the notes.

Ruth will play at a school program tonight. She puts on her

best _____ so she will look nice. It is the color of a

_____ sky. Her father says she looks _____ .

There is a _____ crowd at the school. Ruth

plays well and everyone claps.

blue	**cute**	**flute**	**huge**	**music**
ruler	**Ruth**	**suit**	**super**	**tune**

Super Reader Award

_____

receives this award for

_____

Keep up the great work!

_____ _____

signed date

Reading Award

_____

receives this award for

_____

Great Job!

_____ _____

signed date

CD-3726

Answer Key

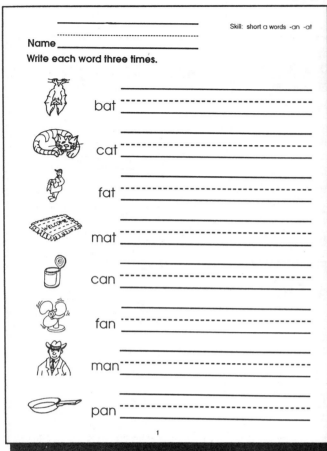

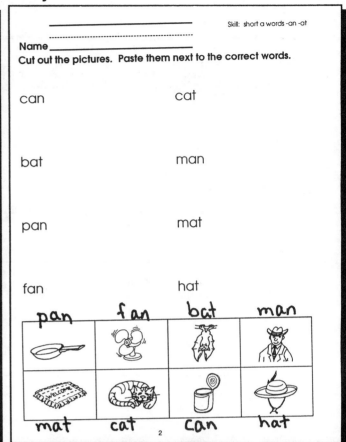

Name _____

Skill: short a words -an -at

Write each word three times.

bat

cat

fat

mat

can

fan

man

pan

1

Name _____

Skill: short a words -an -at

Cut out the pictures. Paste them next to the correct words.

can   cat

bat   man

pan   mat

fan   hat

pan	fan	bat	man
mat	cat	can	hat

2

Name _____

Skill: short a words -an -at

Unscramble the words and write them on the lines.

t m a t	a h t
mat	hat
a n m	p n a
man	pan
n f a	a c t
fan	cat
t a b	n a c
bat	can

Circle the words that are not used above.

(fat)   (ban)   (rat)   can   man
fan   mat   cat   bat   (van)
hat   (sat)   pan   (tan) (ran)

3

Name _____

Skill: short a words -ag -all

Write each word three times.

bag

rag

tag

wag

ball

fall

tall

wall

4

© 1996 Kelley Wingate Publications   106   CD-3726

Answer Key

Name _____

Skill: short a words -ag -all

Cut out the pictures. Paste them next to the correct words.

fall

tag

bag

tall

wall

wag

ball

rag

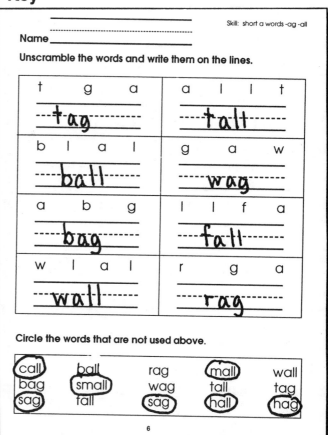

Name _____

Skill: short a words -ag -all

Unscramble the words and write them on the lines.

t g a	a l l t
tag	*talt*
b l a l	g a w
ball	*wag*
a b g	l f a
bag	*fall*
w l a l	r g a
wall	*rag*

Circle the words that are not used above.

(call) ball rag (mall) wall

bag (small) wag tall tag

(sag) fall (sag) (hall) (hag)

6

Name _____

Skill: short e words -en -et

Write each word three times.

hen _____

men _____

pen _____

ten _____

jet _____

net _____

pet _____

wet _____

7

Name _____

Skill: short e words -en -et

Cut out the pictures. Paste them next to the correct words.

pet

men

ten

jet

wet

hen

pen

net

jet *pen* *pet* *wet*

men *hen* *net* *ten*

8

Answer Key

Name

Skill: short e words -en -et

Unscramble the words and write them on the lines.

t j e	p n e
jet	**pen**
t e p	e n t
pet	**net/ten**
n m e	e w t
men	**wet**
n e h	n t e
hen	**ten/net**

Circle the words that are not used above.

jet	(den)	(Ben)	wet	men
ten	pen	net	(them)	pet
(set)	(met)	(bet)	hen	(get)

9

Name

Skill: short e words -ed -ell

Write each word three times.

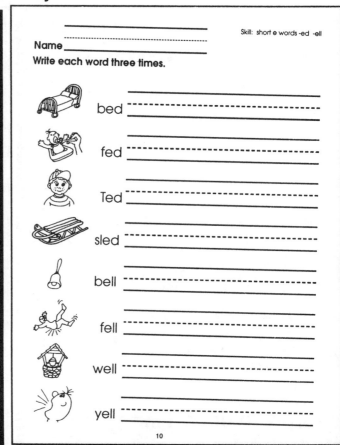

bed _____

fed _____

Ted _____

sled _____

bell _____

fell _____

well _____

yell _____

10

Name

Skill: short e words -ed -ell

Cut out the pictures. Paste them next to the correct words.

sled   well

bell   fed

bed   yell

fell   Ted

fed   well   bed   Ted

yell   sled   bell   fell

11

Name

Skill: short e words -ed -ell

Unscramble the words and write them on the lines.

e s l d	e l y l
sled	**yell**
l f e l	b d e
fell	**bed**
d e r	b l e l
red	**belt**
l l w e	e d f
well	**fed**

Circle the words that are not used above.

(Ted)	red	(led)	well	bed
sled	bell	(sell)	fell	(cell)
(tell)	fed	(Ned)	(wed)	yell

12

---

108   CD-3726

Answer Key

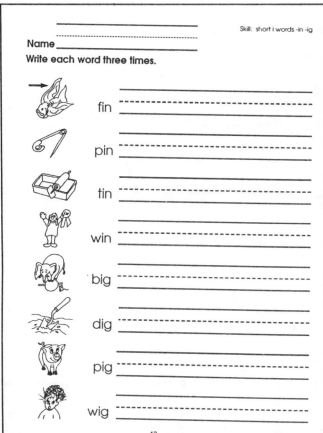

Answer Key

Worksheet 17

Name _____

Skill: short i words -ip -ill

Cut out the pictures. Paste them next to the correct words.

lip   fill

hill   hip

rip   bill

pill   zip

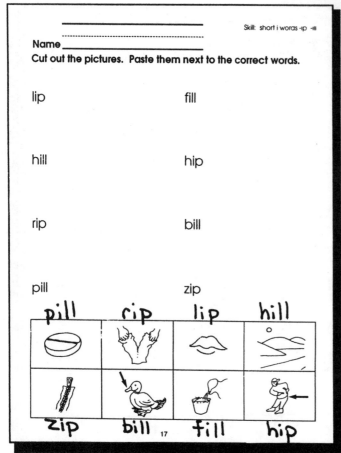

pill	rip	lip	hill
zip	bill 17	fill	hip

Worksheet 18

Name _____

Skill: short i words -ip -ill

Unscramble the words and write them on the lines.

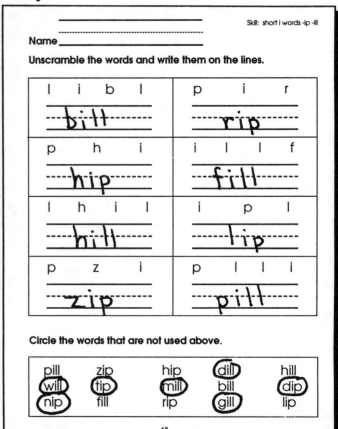

l i b l	p i r
bill	rip
p h i	i l l f
hip	fill
l h i l	i p l
hill	lip
p z i	p l l i
zip	pill

Circle the words that are not used above.

pill	zip	hip	dill	hill
will	tip	mill	bill	dip
nip	fill	rip	gill	lip

18

Worksheet 19

Name _____

Skill: short o words -ot -op

Write each word three times.

cot _____

dot _____

hot _____

pot _____

hop _____

mop _____

pop _____

top _____

19

Worksheet 20

Name _____

Skill: short o words -ot -op

Cut out the pictures. Paste them next to the correct words.

hot   hop

mop   dot

cot   top

pop   pot

pot	mop	cot	dot
hop	top 20	hot	pop

CD-3726

Answer Key

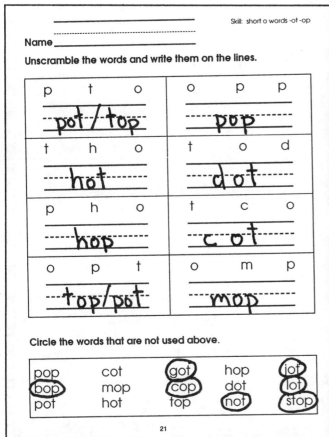

Name _____

Skill: short o words -ot -op

Unscramble the words and write them on the lines.

p t o	o p p
pot/top	pop
t h o	t o d
hot	dot
p h o	t c o
hop	cot
o p t	o m p
top/pot	mop

Circle the words that are not used above.

pop	cot	(got)	hop	(jot)
(bop)	mop	(cop)	dot	(lot)
pot	hot	top	(not)	(stop)

21

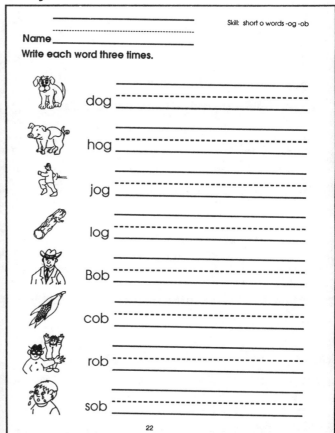

Name _____

Skill: short o words -og -ob

Write each word three times.

dog _____

hog _____

jog _____

log _____

Bob _____

cob _____

rob _____

sob _____

22

Name _____

Skill: short o words -og -ob

Cut out the pictures. Paste them next to the correct words.

cob   hog

log   rob

Bob   jog

dog   sob

jog	Bob	dog	cob
log	rob	sob	hog

23

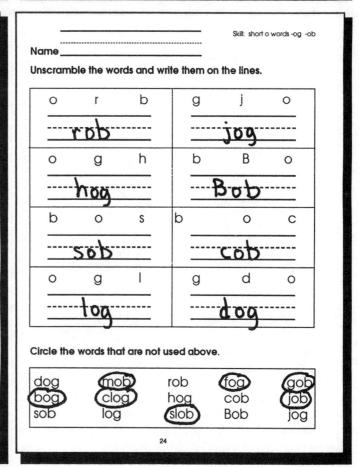

Name _____

Skill: short o words -og -ob

Unscramble the words and write them on the lines.

o r b	g j o
rob	jog
o g h	b B o
hog	Bob
b o s	b o c
sob	cob
o g l	g d o
log	dog

Circle the words that are not used above.

dog	(mob)	rob	(fog)	(gob)
(bog)	(clog)	hog	cob	(job)
sob	log	(slob)	Bob	jog

24

© 1996 Kelley Wingate Publications   111   CD-3726

Answer Key

Name _____

Write each word three times.

cub

rub

sub

tub

bug

jug

rug

tug

25

Name _____

Cut out the pictures. Paste them next to the correct words.

bug   tub

sub   jug

rug   rub

cub   tug

tub	jug	cub	tug
rug	sub	bug	rub

26

Name _____

Unscramble the words and write them on the lines.

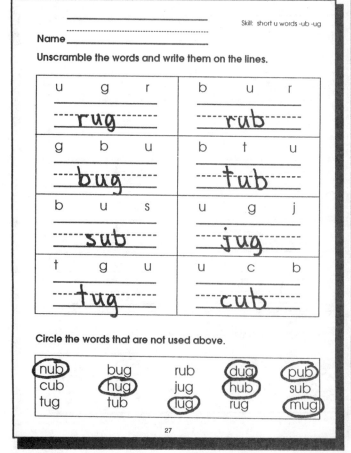

u g r	b u r
rug	rub
g b u	b t u
bug	tub
b u s	u g j
sub	jug
t g u	u c b
tug	cub

Circle the words that are not used above.

(nub)   bug   rub   (dug)   (pub)
cub   (hug)   jug   (hub)   sub
tug   tub   (lug)   rug   (mug)

27

Name _____

Write each word three times.

gum

drum

mum

plum

bump

hump

jump

pump

28

Answer Key

Page 29

_____

Name _____

Skill: short u words -um -ump

Cut out the pictures. Paste them next to the correct words.

jump   drum

gum   bump

hump   plum

mum   pump

jump   drum   pump   hump

gum   plum ₂₉   bump   mum

Page 30

_____

Name _____

Skill: short u words -um -ump

Unscramble the words and write them on the lines.

m l u p	p u p **m**
plum	pump
m u j p	m u g
jump	gum
u m d r	p m b u
drum	bump
m m u	m u h p
mum	hump

Circle the words that are not used above.

plum   drum   dump   jump   bum
bump   chum   lump   gum   sum
stump   hump   mum   hum   pump

30

Page 31

_____

Name _____

Skill: long a words -ace -ake

Write each word three times.

face _____

lace _____

race _____

space _____

bake _____

cake _____

lake _____

rake _____

31

Page 32

_____

Name _____

Skill: long a words -ace -ake

Cut out the pictures. Match them to the words and paste.

space   rake

cake   lace

race   bake

lake   face

face   cake   bake   lace

rake   space ₃₂   lake   race

Answer Key

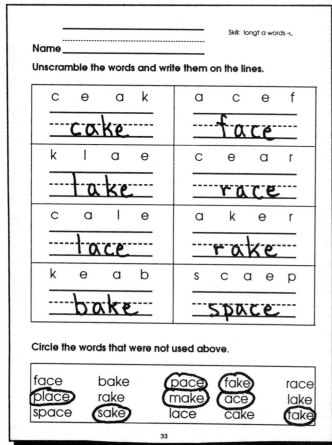

Skill: longt a words -c

Name _____

Unscramble the words and write them on the lines.

c e a k	a c e f
cake	face
k l a e	c e a r
take	race
c a l e	a k e r
face	rake
k e a b	s c a e p
bake	space

Circle the words that were not used above.

face   bake   (pace) (fake)   race
(place)   rake   (make) (ace)   lake
space   (sake)   lace   cake   (take)

33

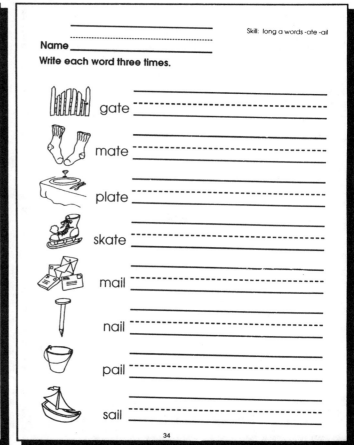

Skill: long a words -ate -ail

Name _____

Write each word three times.

gate _____

mate _____

plate _____

skate _____

mail _____

nail _____

pail _____

sail _____

34

Skill: long a words -ate -ail

Name _____

Cut out the pictures. Match them to the words and paste.

pail   mate

skate   mail

nail   plate

gate   sail

pail	plate	gate	mail
nail	skate	mate	sail

35

Skill: long a words -ate -ail

Name _____

Unscramble the words and write them on the lines.

t e m a	a n i l
mate	nail
a p l i	l a s i
pail	sail
t l a p e	t a g e
plate	gate
m a l i	k a s t e
mail	skate

Circle the words that were not used above.

skate   mail   (date) (fate) (late)
(hate)   sail   gate (bail) (fail)
plate   (nail)   mate   nail   pail

36

CD-3726

Page 37

_____

Skill: long e words -eam -ear

Name_____

Write each word three times.

beam _____

dream _____

seam _____

team _____

fear _____

hear _____

tear _____

ear _____

37

Page 38

_____

Skill: long e words -eam -ear

Name_____

Cut out the pictures. Match them to the words and paste.

seam   hear

ear   team

dream   fear

tear   beam

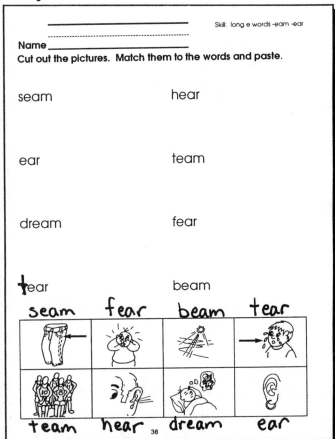

seam   fear   beam   tear

team   hear   dream   ear

38

Page 39

_____

Skill: long e words -eam -ear

Name_____

Unscramble the words and write them on the lines.

r e t a	a e s m
tear	seam
r e a f	m e a r d
fear	dream
y r e a	a h e r
year	hear
t a e m	m a e b
team	beam

Circle the words that were not used above.

fear   (cream)   seam   (gear)   (near)
(dear)   beam   (steam)   year   (ear)
dream   hear   tear   (clear)   team

39

Page 40

_____

Skill: long e words -eed -eep

Name_____

Write each word three times.

reed _____

seed _____

speed _____

weed _____

deep _____

jeep _____

sheep _____

sleep _____

40

115

CD-3726

Answer Key

Name

Skill: long e words -eed -eep

Name

Cut out the pictures. Match them to the words and paste.

seed   jeep

sheep   speed

weed   deep

sleep   reed

reed   **deep**   **sheep**   **speed**

seed   **sleep**₄₁   **jeep**   **weed**

Name

Skill: long e words -eed -eep

Unscramble the words and write them on the lines.

e e h s p	e e s d
sheep	**seed**
e p d e	d e r e
deep	**reed**
s e p e d	w e d e
speed	**weed**
l e p e s	p e j e
sleep	**jeep**

Circle the words that were not used above.

weed (deed) deep (keep) seed
(feed) speed (peep) (need) (seep)
(need) sheep reed sleep jeep

42

Name

Skill: long i words -ice -ine

Write each word three times.

dice _____

mice _____

rice _____

price _____

line _____

nine _____

pine _____

vine _____

43

Name

Skill: long i words -ice -ine

Cut out the pictures. Match them to the words and paste.

line   rice

dice   pine

nine   price

mice   vine

vine   **line**   **dice**   **mice**

price   **rice**₄₄   **pine**   **nine**

---

116   CD-3726

Answer Key

Page 45

Name _____

Skill: long i words -ice -ine

Unscramble the words and write them on the lines.

n e v i	c r i e
vine	rice
d e i c	i n n e
dice	nine
n i p e	p i e r c
pine	price
i c e m	n i l e
mice	line

Circle the words that were not used above.

pine (fine) dice (nice) (mine)
(ice) line (slice) (wine) vine
price (dine) nine mice rice

45

Page 46

Name _____

Skill: long i words -ive -ide

Write each word three times.

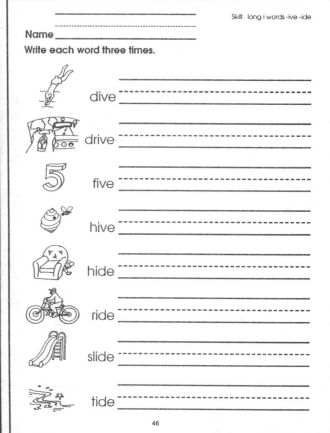

dive _____

drive _____

five _____

hive _____

hide _____

ride _____

slide _____

tide _____

46

Page 47

Name _____

Skill: long i words -ive -ide

Cut out the pictures. Match them to the words and paste.

tide   hive

drive   hide

ride   five

dive   slide

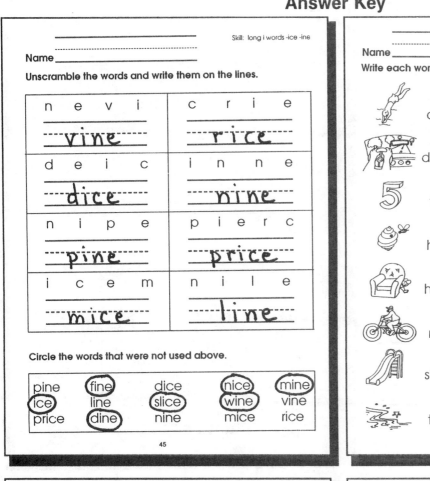

drive   hive   slide   ride

dive   five   tide   hide

47

Page 48

Name _____

Skill: long i words -ive -ide

Unscramble the words and write them on the lines.

d i l s e	v i f e
slide	five
e d i w	d i r e
wide	ride
e v i h	v i r e d
hive	drive
d i e h	e i v d
hide	dive

Circle the words that were not used above.

wide hive (live) (pride) (alive)
(side) five slide (tide) dive
drive ride (bride) hide (chive)

48

117

CD-3726

Answer Key

Name _____
Skill: long o words -oat -old

Write each word three times.

boat _____

coat _____

goat _____

moat _____

cold _____

fold _____

gold _____

hold _____

49

Name _____
Skill: long o words -o-

Cut out the pictures. Match them to the words and paste.

gold   goat

boat   fold

hold   moat

coat   cold

coat **boat** **goat** **moat**

hold **gold** **cold** **fold**

50

Name _____
Skill: long o words -oat -old

Unscramble the words and write them on the lines.

t o c a	d o l f
coat	**fold**

a t o b	o a t m
boat	**moat**

o l d h	l o c d
hold	**cold**

t o a g	d o l g
goat	**gold**

Circle the words that were not used above.

(float)   gold   (oat)   moat   cold
boat   (told)   coat   hold   (bold)
(mold)   fold   goat   (sold) (old)

51

Name _____
Skill: long o words -one -ore

Write each word three times.

bone _____

cone _____

phone _____

stone _____

core _____

tore _____

shore _____

store _____

52

© 1996 Kelley Wingate Publications   118   CD-3726

Answer Key

Name _____
Skill: long o words -one -ore

Cut out the pictures. Match them to the words and paste.

tore   phone

bone   store

core   stone

cone   shore

tore	phone	store	cone
bone	stone	shore	core

Name _____
Skill: long o words -one -ore

Unscramble the words and write them on the lines.

n o p h e	r o c e
phone	core
o n c e	t r o e
cone	tore
s o h e r	o n s e t
shore	stone
o r t e s	n e o b
store	bone

Circle the words that were not used above.

bone	more	pore	lore	stone
core	cone	shore	lone	tone
phone	tore	sore	store	bore

54

Name _____
Skill: long u words u sound

Write each word three times.

cube _____

flute _____

fruit _____

fuel _____

huge _____

mule _____

music _____

ruler _____

55

Name _____
Skill: long u words u sound

Cut out the pictures. Match them to the words and paste.

fuel   flute

music   ruler

mule   cube

huge   fruit

music	mule	fruit	flute
ruler	huge	fuel	cube

56

---

119   CD-3726

Answer Key

Page 57

Skill: long u words u sound

Name

Unscramble the words and write them on the lines.

u h g e	l u e m
huge	mule
t i u f r	t u c e
fruit	cute
b c e u	s c u i m
cube	music
l e f u	l e r u r
fuel	ruler

Circle the words that were not used above.

fuel   cube   (use)   fruit   (rule)
(fume)   music   (fuse)   ruler   mule
(future)   cute   huge   (fume)   (plume)

Page 58

Skill: long u words oo sound

Name

Write each word three times.

blue
cute
glue
prune
suit
super
tube
tune

Page 59

Skill: long u words oo sound

Name

Cut out the pictures. Match them to the words and paste.

tune   glue

super   prune

blue   tube

cute   suit

tune   glue   cute   blue

prune   suit   tube   super

Page 60

Skill: long u words oo sound

Name

Unscramble the words and write them on the lines.

t n u e	u l g e
tune	glue
p r u s e	n u p r e
super	prune
e u b l	u i t s
blue	suit
b u t e	t u f l e
tube	flute

Circle the words that were not used above.

flute   (tuna)   (ruin)   glue   prune
(dune)   (rude)   tune   (duty)   (future)
suit   tube   blue   (human)   super

© 1996 Kelley Wingate Publications   120   CD-3726

Answer Key

Page 61

Name _____

Skill: identify short vowel a e i o u

Write the missing vowel for each picture.

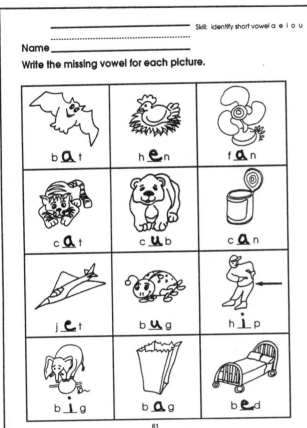

b **a** t	h **e** n	f **a** n
c **a** t	c **u** b	c **a** n
j **e** t	b **u** g	h **i** p
b **i** g	b **a** g	b **e** d

61

Page 62

Name _____

Skill: identify short vowel a e i o u

Write the missing vowel for each picture.

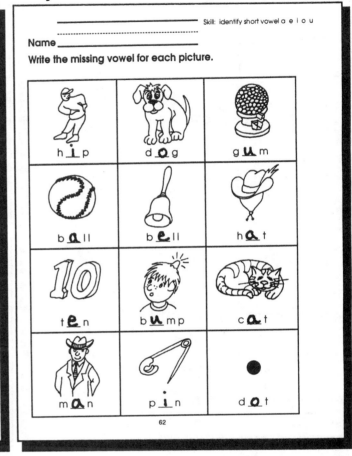

h **i** p	d **o** g	g **u** m
b **a** ll	b **e** ll	h **a** t
t **e** n	b **u** mp	c **a** t
m **a** n	p **i** n	d **o** t

62

Page 63

Name _____

Skill: identify short vowel a e i o u

Write the missing vowel for each picture.

r **u** b	f **a** n	n **e** t
d **o** g	m **o** p	j **u** g
r **a** g	f **e** d	l **i** p
h **o** g	dr **u** m	f **e** ll **a**

63

Page 64

Name _____

Skill: identify short vowel a e i o u

Write the missing vowel for each picture.

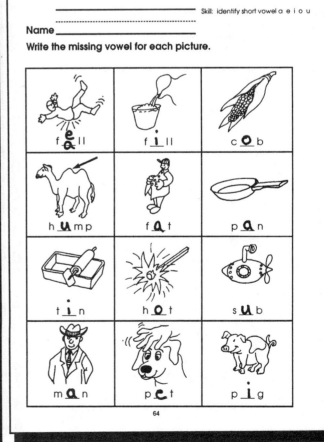

f **e** ll **a**	f **i** ll	c **o** b
h **u** mp	f **a** t	p **a** n
t **i** n	h **o** t	s **u** b
m **a** n	p **e** t	p **i** g

64

CD-3726

Answer Key

Name _____ Skill: identify short vowel a e i o u

Write the missing vowel for each picture.

p**o**p	r**u**g	t**a**g
r**e**d	r**i**p	j**u**g
m**u**m	t**a**ll	w**a**ll
h**i**ll	r**o**b	j**u**mp

65

Name _____ Skill: identify long vowel a e i o u

Write the missing vowel for each picture.

f**a**ce	b**e**am	d**i**ce
b**o**at	c**u**be	b**a**ke
f**e**ar	l**i**ne	c**o**ld
h**u**ge	g**a**te	r**e**ed

66

Name _____ Skill: identify long vowel a e i o u

Write the missing vowel for each picture.

d**i**ve	b**o**ne	bl**u**e
m**a**il	d**e**ep	h**i**de
c**o**re	s**u**it	l**a**ce
dr**e**am	m**i**ce	c**o**at

67

Name _____ Skill: identify long vowel a e i o

Write the missing vowel for each picture.

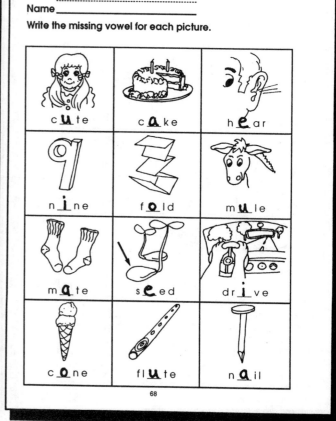

c**u**te	c**a**ke	h**e**ar
n**i**ne	f**o**ld	m**u**le
m**a**te	s**e**ed	dr**i**ve
c**o**ne	fl**u**te	n**a**il

68

122

CD-3726

Answer Key

Skill: identify long vowel a e i o u

Name_____

Write the missing vowel for each picture.

j **e** ep	r **i** de	t **o** re
s **u** per	r **a** ce	s **e** am
r **i** ce	g **o** at	fr **u** it
l **a** ke	t **e** ar	p **i** ne

69

Skill: identify long vowel a e i o u

Name_____

Write the missing vowel for each picture.

g **o** ld	m **u** sic	sp **e** ed
f **i** ve	ph **o** ne	gl **u** e
p **a** il	sh **e** ep	sl **i** de
c **o** re	t **u** be	pl **a** te

70

Skill: identify the vowel a e i o u

Name_____

Write the missing vowel for each picture.

w **i** n	sp **a** ce	p **o** t
t **e** am	t **u** b	pr **i** ce
p **a** n	m **o** at	w **e** t
f **u** el	w **i** g	r **a** ke

71

Skill: identify the vowel a e i o u

Name_____

Write the missing vowel for each picture.

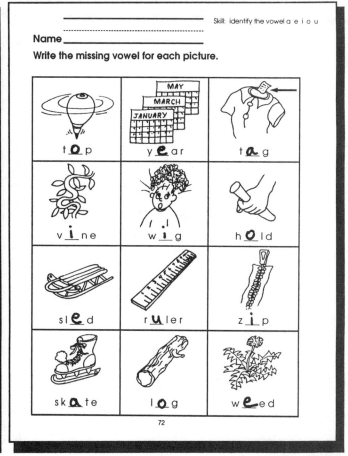

t **o** p	y **e** ar	t **a** g
v **i** ne	w **i** g	h **o** ld
sl **e** d	r **u** ler	z **i** p
sk **a** te	l **o** g	w **e** ed

72

123   CD-3726

Answer Key

Name _____
Skill: identify the vowel a e i o u

Write the missing vowel for each picture.

pl**u**m	h**i**ve	w**e**ll
st**o**ne	y**e**ll	pr**u**ne
p**i**ll	s**a**il	s**o**b
sl**e**ep	p**u**mp	st**o**re

73

Name _____
Skill: use in context short a

Choose the answer that makes sense then write it on the line.

1. A **bat** can fly.   (bat)   cat
2. Please **rub** my back.   rib   (rub)
3. That **man** is my father.   men   (man)
4. It is **hot** today.   (hot)   hat
5. Put the lunch in a **bag**.   big   (bag)
6. I will **jog** to school.   (jog)   jug
7. Some apples are **red**.   (red)   rod
8. Play **ball** with me.   (ball)   bell
9. My **pet** is a dog.   pat   (pet)
10. The puppy will **wag** his tail.   wig   (wag)

Write the answers that have a short a sound here.

bat   man   bag   pat
cat   hat   ball   wag

74

Name _____
Skill: use in context short a

Choose the answer that makes sense then write it on the line.

1. Do not **fall** down!   (fall)   fell
2. A fish has a **fin**.   fun   (fin)
3. A **rat** ate the cheese.   sat   (rat)
4. Do not **rip** my paper.   (rip)   lip
5. A **fan** makes wind.   fin   (fan)
6. A camel has one **hump**.   (hump)   jump
7. A rabbit can **hop**.   (hop)   hip
8. I can **dig** a big hole.   (dig)   dug
9. I play a **drum** in the band.   gum   (drum)
10. I will **win** the race.   won   (win)

Write the answers that have a short a sound here.

fall   rat
sat   fan

75

Name _____
Skill: use in context short e

Choose the answer that makes sense then write it on the line.

1. The **rug** is on the floor.   (rug)   rag
2. Are you feeling **well**?   (well)   will
3. That is a **tall** tree.   tell   (tall)
4. A **jet** flys over clouds.   jot   (jet)
5. The **hen** has two chicks.   (hen)   men
6. Spot is the name of my **dog**.   dig   (dog)
7. I got **wet** in the rain.   (wet)   met
8. **Fill** my cup to the top.   (Fill)   Fall
9. I will go to **bed** now.   (bed)   bad
10. Fry the eggs in that **pan**.   pin   (pan)

Write the answers that have a short e sound here.

well   jet   men   met
tell   hen   wet   bed

76

---

   124   CD-3726

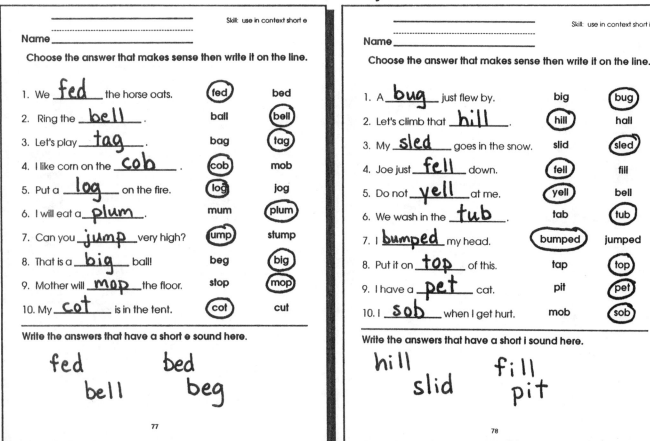

Name _____
Skill: use in context short e

Choose the answer that makes sense then write it on the line.

1. We **fed** the horse oats. (fed) bed
2. Ring the **bell** . ball (bell)
3. Let's play **tag** . bag (tag)
4. I like corn on the **cob** . (cob) mob
5. Put a **log** on the fire. (log) jog
6. I will eat a **plum** . mum (plum)
7. Can you **jump** very high? (ump) stump
8. That is a **big** ball! beg (big)
9. Mother will **mop** the floor. stop (mop)
10. My **cot** is in the tent. (cot) cut

Write the answers that have a short e sound here.

fed   bed
   bell   beg

77

Name _____
Skill: use in context short i

Choose the answer that makes sense then write it on the line.

1. A **bug** just flew by. big (bug)
2. Let's climb that **hill** . (hill) hall
3. My **sled** goes in the snow. slid (sled)
4. Joe just **fell** down. (fell) fill
5. Do not **yell** at me. (yell) bell
6. We wash in the **tub** . tab (tub)
7. I **bumped** my head. (bumped) jumped
8. Put it on **top** of this. tap (top)
9. I have a **pet** cat. pit (pet)
10. I **sob** when I get hurt. mob (sob)

Write the answers that have a short i sound here.

hill   fill
   slid   pit

78

Name _____
Skill: use in context short o

Choose the answer that makes sense then write it on the line.

1. A **pill** can make you well. hill (pill)
2. Put a **dot** over the letter i. pot (dot)
3. The dog **tugs** on a rope. bugs (tugs)
4. **Zip** the zipper. (Zip) Sip
5. A **hip** is part of a leg. (hip) hop
6. This old shirt is a **rag** . (rag) rig
7. I have **ten** toes. tin (ten)
8. I like to drink **pop** . pup (pop)
9. Cook soup in a big **pot** . pet (pot)
10. That lady wears a **wig** . wag (wig)

Write the answers that have a short o sound here.

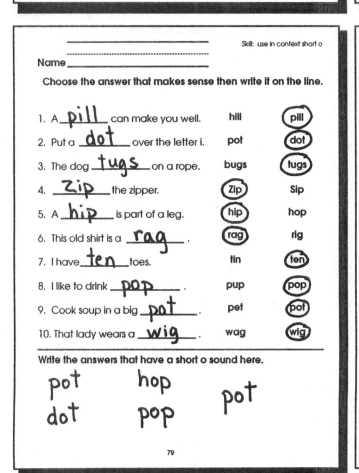

pot   hop
dot   pop   pot

79

Name _____
Skill: use in context short u

Choose the answer that makes sense then write it on the line.

1. A **pig** is an animal. (pig) peg
2. I bit my **lip** ! lap (lip)
3. A **mum** is a flower (mum) gum
4. A **cub** is a baby bear. (cub) cab
5. Boys grow up to be **men** . (men) hen
6. I blow bubbles with **gum** . (gum) hum
7. I have a butterfly **net** . (net) nut
8. Use a **pen** , not a pencil. ten (pen)
9. A **sub** goes under water. sob (sub)
10. **Pump** air into my bike tires. (Pump) Lump

Write the answers that have a short u sound here.

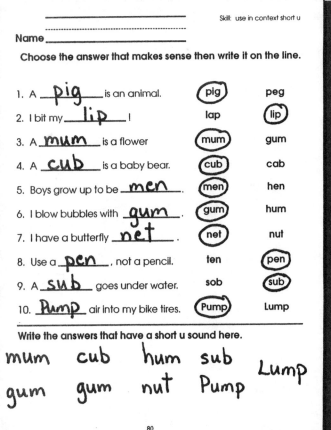

mum   cub   hum   sub
   gum   gum   nut   Pump   Lump

80

125   CD-3726

Answer Key

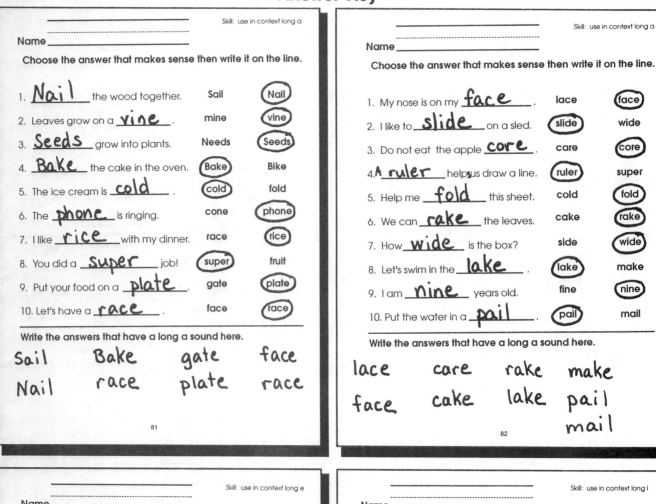

Worksheet 1 (page 81) — Skill: use in context long a

Name _____

Choose the answer that makes sense then write it on the line.

1. **Nail** the wood together. — Sail — (Nail)
2. Leaves grow on a **vine**. — mine — (vine)
3. **Seeds** grow into plants. — Needs — (Seeds)
4. **Bake** the cake in the oven. — (Bake) — Bike
5. The ice cream is **cold**. — (cold) — fold
6. The **phone** is ringing. — cone — (phone)
7. I like **rice** with my dinner. — race — (rice)
8. You did a **super** job! — (super) — fruit
9. Put your food on a **plate**. — gate — (plate)
10. Let's have a **race**. — face — (race)

Write the answers that have a long a sound here.

Sail   Bake   gate   face
Nail   race   plate   race

81

Worksheet 2 (page 82) — Skill: use in context long a

Name _____

Choose the answer that makes sense then write it on the line.

1. My nose is on my **face**. — lace — (face)
2. I like to **slide** on a sled. — (slide) — wide
3. Do not eat the apple **core**. — care — (core)
4. A **ruler** helps us draw a line. — (ruler) — super
5. Help me **fold** this sheet. — cold — (fold)
6. We can **rake** the leaves. — cake — (rake)
7. How **wide** is the box? — side — (wide)
8. Let's swim in the **lake**. — (lake) — make
9. I am **nine** years old. — fine — (nine)
10. Put the water in a **pail**. — (pail) — mail

Write the answers that have a long a sound here.

lace   care   rake   make
face   cake   lake   pail
  mail

82

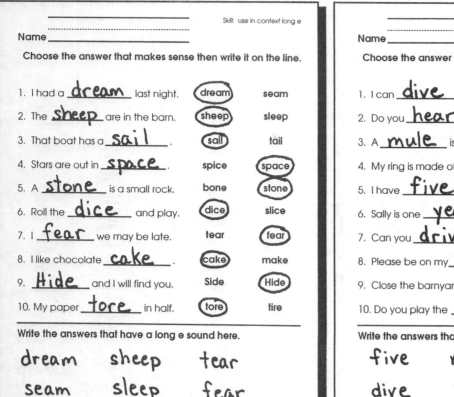

Worksheet 3 (page 83) — Skill: use in context long e

Name _____

Choose the answer that makes sense then write it on the line.

1. I had a **dream** last night. — (dream) — seam
2. The **sheep** are in the barn. — (sheep) — sleep
3. That boat has a **sail**. — (sail) — tail
4. Stars are out in **space**. — spice — (space)
5. A **stone** is a small rock. — bone — (stone)
6. Roll the **dice** and play. — (dice) — slice
7. I **fear** we may be late. — tear — (fear)
8. I like chocolate **cake**. — (cake) — make
9. **Hide** and I will find you. — Side — (Hide)
10. My paper **tore** in half. — (tore) — tire

Write the answers that have a long e sound here.

dream   sheep   tear
seam   sleep   fear

83

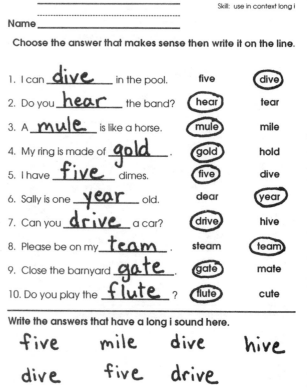

Worksheet 4 (page 84) — Skill: use in context long i

Name _____

Choose the answer that makes sense then write it on the line.

1. I can **dive** in the pool. — five — (dive)
2. Do you **hear** the band? — (hear) — tear
3. A **mule** is like a horse. — (mule) — mile
4. My ring is made of **gold**. — (gold) — hold
5. I have **five** dimes. — (five) — dive
6. Sally is one **year** old. — dear — (year)
7. Can you **drive** a car? — (drive) — hive
8. Please be on my **team**. — steam — (team)
9. Close the barnyard **gate**. — (gate) — mate
10. Do you play the **flute**? — (flute) — cute

Write the answers that have a long i sound here.

five   mile   dive   hive
dive   five   drive

84

Answer Key

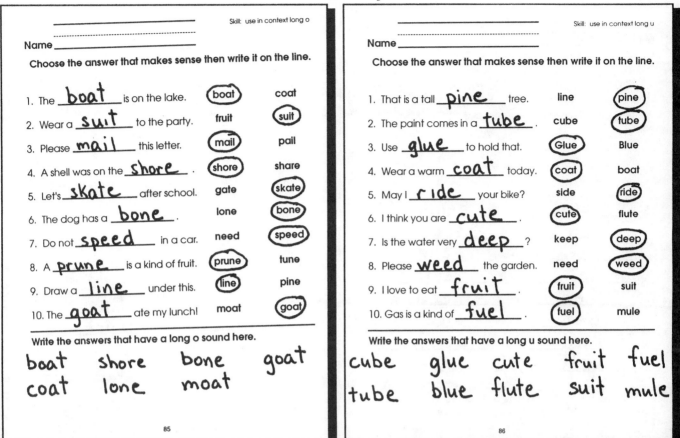

Name _____ Skill: use in context long o

Choose the answer that makes sense then write it on the line.

1. The __boat__ is on the lake. (boat) coat
2. Wear a __suit__ to the party. fruit (suit)
3. Please __mail__ this letter. (mail) pail
4. A shell was on the __shore__. (shore) share
5. Let's __skate__ after school. gate (skate)
6. The dog has a __bone__. lone (bone)
7. Do not __speed__ in a car. need (speed)
8. A __prune__ is a kind of fruit. (prune) tune
9. Draw a __line__ under this. (line) pine
10. The __goat__ ate my lunch! moat (goat)

Write the answers that have a long o sound here.

boat shore bone goat
coat lone moat

85

Name _____ Skill: use in context long u

Choose the answer that makes sense then write it on the line.

1. That is a tall __pine__ tree. line (pine)
2. The paint comes in a __tube__. cube (tube)
3. Use __glue__ to hold that. (Glue) Blue
4. Wear a warm __coat__ today. (coat) boat
5. May I __ride__ your bike? side (ride)
6. I think you are __cute__. (cute) flute
7. Is the water very __deep__? keep (deep)
8. Please __weed__ the garden. need (weed)
9. I love to eat __fruit__. (fruit) suit
10. Gas is a kind of __fuel__. (fuel) mule

Write the answers that have a long u sound here.

cube glue cute fruit fuel
tube blue flute suit mule

86

Name _____ Skill: use in context long u

Choose the answer that makes sense then write it on the line.

1. I shop in that __store__. (store) core
2. I like to listen to __music__. ruler (music)
3. The cat does not like __mice__. price (mice)
4. I need an ice __cube__. (cube) cute
5. The bees are in their __hive__. drive (hive)
6. __Hold__ on to my hand. Gold (Hold)
7. I like the color __blue__. (blue) glue
8. That shirt is __huge__ on you! (huge) tube
9. I __sleep__ in a bed. sheep (sleep)
10. Play a __tune__ on your horn. (tune) prune

Write the answers that have a long u sound here.

ruler cube blue huge tune
music cute glue tube prune

87

Name _____ Skill: categorize long and short a

Put these words into the correct group.

bag	bat	bake	cake
can	fan	face	gate
mate	nail	pan	rag
rake	space	tall	wall

Short a	Long a
bag	bake
bat	cake
can	face
fan	gate
pan	mate
rag	nail
tall	rake
wall	space

Choose five words and draw a picture next to each.

88

© 1996 Kelley Wingate Publications   127   CD-3726

Answer Key

_____ Skill: categorize long and short e

Name_____

Put these words into the correct group.

beam	bed	deep	fear
fell	hen	jeep	jet
men	pet	reed	sled
sleep	team	year	yell

Short e	Long e
bed	beam
fell	deep
hen	fear
jet	jeep
men	reed
pet	sleep
sled	team
yell	year

Choose five words and draw a picture next to each.

89

_____ Skill: categorize long and short i

Name_____

Put these words into the correct group.

bill	dice	dig	dive
fin	five	hide	hill
line	lip	pin	price
vine	wide	wig	zip

Short i	Long i
bill	dice
dig	dive
fin	five
hill	hide
lip	line
pin	price
wig	vine
zip	wide

Choose five words and draw a picture next to each.

90

_____ Skill: categorize long and short o

Name_____

Put these words into the correct group.

boat	cob	cone	dot
fold	goat	hold	hop
jog	log	moat	mop
phone	pot	rob	store

Short o	Long o
cob	boat
dot	cone
hop	fold
jog	goat
log	hold
mop	moat
pot	phone
rob	store

Choose five words and draw a picture next to each.

91

_____ Skill: categorize long and short u

Name_____

Put these words into the correct group.

blue	bug	cub	cute
drum	flute	fruit	glue
gum	hump	jug	mule
rub	ruler	tug	tune

Short u	Long u
bug	blue
cub	cute
drum	flute
gum	fruit
hump	glue
jug	mule
rub	ruler
tug	tune

Choose five words and draw a picture next to each.

92

Answer Key

Name _____ Skill: categorize long/short a/e

Put these words into the correct group.

ball	bell	cat	dream
fed	hear	lake	man
net	pail	race	sheep
skate	ten	wag	weed

Short a
ball
cat
man
wag

Short e
bell
fed
net
ten

Long a
lake
pail
race
skate

Long e
dream
hear
sheep
weed

93

Name _____ Skill: categorize long/short o/u

Put these words into the correct group.

bone	bump	coat	core
cot	cube	dog	huge
mule	plum	rug	sob
stone	suit	top	tub

Short o
cot
dog
sob
top

Short u
bump
plum
rug
tub

Long o
bone
coat
core
stone

Long u
cube
huge
mule
suit

94

Name _____ Skill: context short a

Fill in the blanks with the short a words in the box.

Sally's Walk

Sally went for a walk down her street. She stopped in front of the house next to hers. A **man** was in the yard. He was feeding his **cat**. The man went into his house. The cat jumped to the top of a brick **wall** that went around the yard. Sally walked on to the next yard. A dog was barking at the cat. He began to **wag** his tail when he saw Sally. He got his **ball** and tossed it in the air. The dog put the ball at Sally's feet and **sat** down. She threw the ball and the dog went after it. He came back with a paper **bag** in his mouth. A **tag** on the bag said "Open Me". He gave the bag to **Sally** and she opened it. **Can** you guess what was inside?

| bag | ball | Can | cat | man |
| Sally | sat | tag | wag | wall |

95

Name _____ Skill: context short e

Fill in the blanks with the short e words at the bottom of the page.

Ned

One summer day Ned went to his uncle's farm. He went to the barnyard to look around. Ned saw a fat **hen** and her five babies. He **fed** corn to the hen. There were some sheep in a **pen** near the barn. A horse and her colt were in the barn. Ned stopped to **pet** the soft nose of the colt. Ned walked out of the barn and saw a round stone wall. He looked over the wall and saw that it was a wishing **well**. Ned bent over to see further into the well and **fell** in! The water was not very deep, but Ned was all **wet**. He began to **yell** for help. Two **men** came running. They used a big **net** to pull him out. Ned laughed and said "I am all right now"!

| fed | fell | hen | men | net |
| pen | pet | well | wet | yell |

96

Answer Key

Name _____

Skill: context short i

Fill in the blanks with the short i words **at** the bottom of the page.

Bill's Pond

Bill was playing in his back yard. He saw a **big**
pile of dirt under a bush. It was an ant **hill** . He had
an idea. He would make a pond for the ants to **swim**
in. The ants could race and see who would **win** . Bill
began to **dig** a small hole next to the ant hill. He
worked on that hole for a long time. When it was ready he
filled the hole with water. The ants came to the
pond but they did not go **in** . Bill laughed at his
silly idea. Ants cannot swim. They do not have
fins like fish. But now they have a nice pond to
look at!

big	dig	filled	fins	hill
in	silly	swim	will	win

97

Name _____

Skill: context short o

Fill in the blanks with the short o words **at** the bottom of the page.

Friends

Bob and Rob are friends. They are alike in many ways.
Both boys like to climb to the **top** of the fence. Then
they **hop** down. They both have a **dog**
for a pet. They even like the same foods. Their favorite food
is corn on the **cob** . Bob and Rob like to drink
hot chocolate in the winter and cold **pop**
in the summer. Both boys like to make things. Once they
made a big **pot** out of clay. Another time they
made a **log** cabin out of sticks. Bob and
Rob have known each other since they were
two years old. They have been friends for a **long**
time!

cob	dog	hop	hot	log
long	pop	pot	Rob	top

98

Name _____

Skill: context short u

Fill in the blanks with the short u words **at** the bottom of the page.

My Toy Box

I have a big box to keep my toys in. It is painted yellow
and green. My box is **full** of toys. At the bottom I
keep an old red **drum** for banging. Next I have three
boats and one **sub** to play with in the **tub** .
On top of them I keep two stuffed animals. One is a camel
with a big **hump** . The other is a small bear
cub . On the top I keep a real animal! It is a
bug with wings and six legs. My toy box is so full I
have to **tug** on the top to open it. Sometimes I pull
the top so hard it flies open and **bumps** my head.
Then I have to **rub** my head to make it feel better.

bug	bumps	cub	drum	full
hump	rub	sub	tub	tug

99

Name _____

Skill: context long a

Fill in the blanks with the long a words **at** the bottom of the page.

Amy's Party

Amy is having a party today. She **mailed** letters
to all her friends last week to tell them about it. Amy has put
on her best dress. It has **lace** all over it. Her
mother has **baked** a **cake** for the
children to eat. They will put the cake on party **plates** .
Amy has **made** many plans for her party. The
children will play **games** . They will have a running
race . They may even **sail** boats on
the nearby pond! The doorbell rings. It is the first guest.
Amy has a big smile on her **face** .

baked	cake	face	games	lace
made	mailed	plates	race	sail

100

     CD-3726

Answer Key

Name

Skill: context long e

Fill in the blanks with the long e words **at** the bottom of the page.

A Dream by the Sea

Last week Lee went camping with her family. They went to a camp by the sea. They knew it was a nice place because they went there last **year**. The camp has a nice beach for swimming. **Lee** likes to swim in water that is not too **deep**. She is not a good swimmer. The family likes to camp by the **sea**. They have a **jeep** to drive over the sand dunes. They **sleep** in a tent. Lee likes to **hear** the waves at night. One night she had a **dream**. She found a large **seed** and planted it. A giant **weed** grew from the seed. It became a sea weed. What a strange dream!

dream	deep	hear	jeep	Lee
sea	seed	sleep	weed	year

101

Name

Skill: context long i

Fill in the blanks with the long i words **at** the bottom of the page.

The Woods

Mike and Ivan like to picnic in the woods. It takes them only **five** minutes to get there. They like to **ride** their **bikes** down the trails. There are many **pine** trees in the woods. Some of them are covered with **vines** that are just right for swinging from. One tree is so **wide** the boys cannot put their arms around it! Mike and Ivan like to **hide** in the bushes and watch for animals. They often see little **mice** gathering seeds. Once they saw some bees going into a large **hive**. The woods are **alive** with small animals that are fun to watch.

alive	bikes	five	hide	hive
pine	mice	ride	vines	wide

102

Name

Skill: context long o

Fill in the blanks with the long o words **at** the bottom of the page.

Gold Fish

Once a boy named Joe lived near a castle. There was a **moat** around the castle and Joe liked to fish there. He had a small **boat** to fish from. The boat **floated** on the water as Joe fished. **Joe** caught one fish each day for his dinner. One winter morning it was very **cold** out. Joe put on his **coat** and went to the moat. His fingers were so cold he could barely **hold** the oars. He pushed away from the **shore** and began to fish. He looked down and saw a shiny **stone** in the water. Joe picked it up and saw that it was a big piece of **gold**. He had found gold instead of a fish. What a lucky day!

boat	coat	cold	floated	gold
hold	Joe	moat	shore	stone

103

Name

Skill: context long u

Fill in the blanks with the long u words **at** the bottom of the page.

Ruth's Flute

Ruth likes school. She loves **music** class better than anything. She plays a **flute** in the band. Her teacher says she is a **super** student. She can play a **tune** without looking at the music! **Ruth** is learning to write her own songs. She uses a **ruler** to make the lines then draws in the notes. Ruth will play at a school program tonight. She puts on her best **suit** so she will look nice. It is the color of a **blue** sky. Her father says she looks **cute**. There is a **huge** crowd at the school. Ruth plays well and everyone claps.

blue	cute	flute	huge	music
ruler	Ruth	suit	super	tune

104

Certificate of Completion

This certificate certifies that

Has completed

Signed

Date

Keep up the Great Work!

_____ earns this award for

_____

You are TERRIFIC!

_____
Signed

_____
Date

Great Success!

_____

earns this award for

_____

I am Proud of You!

_____
Signed

_____
Date

You Did It!

_____ earns this award for

_____

Keep Up The The Great Work!

_____ Signed

_____ Date

Congratulations!

_____

Receives this award for

_____

Keep up the great work!

_____

Signed

_____

Date

Great Job!

Receives this award for

_____

Keep up the great work!

_____

Signed

_____

Date

Keep up the Great Work!

_____ earns this award for

_____

You are TERRIFIC!

Signed _____

Date _____